Hymns to the Great God

(And Other Spiritual Poems)

By

Johnathan Abraham Antelept

Table of Contents

To Ultimate Love, Oneness, and Maat…
Do Maat, Spread Maat, and Praise the Great God.

Eternal Dawn

He walked by the rivers,
And glowed with the dawn.
Clear as the rivers,
Clear as the quartz.

He walked by the rivers,
Dawning in his mind.
Clearly seen…
Not even once removed.
Self-consciousness was simply *conscious*.

Work was not even once removed.
His hands took stones and sharpened them.

Words were not even once removed,
But came from that in union.

He saw his siblings,
His lover, mother and father,
He saw each one, not once removed.

He saw the strangers from the North
And the strangers from the South,
Not once removed.

The soil and seed,
Not once removed.
The trees and fauna,
Not once removed.
Stone and Sun were One.

The Dawn of his eyes shown to them,
Walking by the rivers clear.

Oh Radiant Child of Dawn!
Oh Radiant Child of Dawn!
Oh Radiant King of the Stars!
Oh Radiant Moon-Faced Govinda!

Oh Radiant Ra is Rising!

The glistening stone unearthed…
Oh Radiant Stone of Kaaba!
Oh Radiant Milk of the Goat Before Buddha Sat Under the Bodhi!
Oh Sling and Stone of David…
The Everfaithful Shepherd!

Oh Radiant eyes of Yosef!
Oh Radiant love of Yahoshua!
Oh Radiant strength of the trunk,
Of the tree of life made stern.

Ra is Rising!
Ra is Rising!
Oh, Radiant Ra is Rising!

Furnish My Home

Furnish my house with linen, silken,
Lentils pasted,
Kisses milken, maidens mellow,
Draped in yellow robes.

Tell me though…for what is lust?
I envy not, nor want in Elohim.
Elders told me: "Patience buck!"
But I kept bucking till my luck was dour.

Time be told, impressed upon my brow, instruction,
And turned me from the battleground,
It led me from destruction.
It came to furnish foyers with fragrances of saffron,
To furnish beds with petals, keeping cups of honey by the bedside…

Kisses milken, maidens mellow,
Draped in yellow robes.
Peace upon the brow of him,
Meditate on Elohim…
Like a fragrance if he utters,
A fragrance mostly silent,
Gently washing through the room.

Furnish my home with wisdom for,
My son to know its truth.
So he shall know, what I knew not,
And he shall need not go towards lust,
But linen silken, draped in roses wreathed.

My son shall know examples of,
A Love Supreme.

He'll see his mother wrapped in kisses,
His sisters shall be mellow bloom,
Wrapped in father's love of them,
And he shall see examples of,
And meditate on peace.

Asiath

Asiath of Asiatic Berry ripe,
Darker than the waning moon
Upon the starless cloudy night.

Eyes of widened cocoa beans,
Coffee bean eyelashes sashing sassafras,
Midnight blue hair that hung
Of ordered forests without dissent...

We stood upon the mountain top,
The vault of sky stretched forth,
A plateau paved on top of it...

I gazed upon the whirling device...
Consternation and a calling.
I could not reach it, falling back,
Falling down upon the ground,
But never losing faith in it.

Asiath, of Berry Riper than the blackened Persian sky,
Slender hands and gracile arm outstretched to help me on my feet,

I took her hand and held it.
Felt her arm was slightly cold, atop the mountain plateau night.
She told me: "Patience...Patience."
Hers like a presence I have yet to know...

Beds of Evergreen

Everlong a river run,
They dreamt of year by year, to come.
Stone and stump,
Rust and grain,
Abandoned towns of Babylon…
They've left for hills
To drink of crystal river water.

Here! Come quickly here!
I've found elixirs bloody ripe!
Take a swig of this, my friend,
Your limbs will loosen limber!

Tidy slippers
Shown to dash
Through dirt and mud
By river yonder…

She sleeps in beds of Evergreen
Awakening with mint tea
And Golden Hymns
From Golden Eagles
Swooping over verdant pastures…

In midday Sun
Her plexus opens
Emanating purely, Presence.
With prescience and patience,
Pouring forth her Golden Breath.

In the Temple

In the temple sits,
In the verdant hills,
Nestled in a mountain cliff,
Ranges of the Ancient Days,
Echoes hymns to Brahma's Brimming,
Everlasting welling light,
Frothing from Eternal Springs,
Resounding Golden Chalice, **Zing!** ...

Filled with darkest berry ripe,
Deeper purpling the hue encompass,
The Blood of Ganga issue forth,
Painting lands with silken silt,
Silkworms grow
And spin from abdomens
Tales of Kingdoms
Left untold...

Our voices raise to rafters oaken,
The Magi flame still never ceases,
Stoking logwood through the night...
Telling tales of kings untold.
Singing hymns to El Elyon.

The Root of Redwood

Everlast
Outlast
The Babylonian Bombasts.

The capital pronouncement,
Unpronounced…

Heal the unhealed.
Shield the unsheltered.

The lands which seep blood,
Give birth to Redwood.

The word which sought to kill,
Only set the faithful compassioned.

The memories fade,
And dreams come and go,
But Elohim stays forever.

Within the Palace of Eternity

Unto the ultimate, prostration,
Of the lesson of Samsara,
EverRising from the wellspring
In sync with creation.
I pray for Absolution,
Absolutely.

Carry me to pure rivers,
By the Bodhi Tree with Buddha,
By Yamuna, Govinda,
And Kaaba in Mecca
With Muhammad and Faithful,
By Gihon with David, Melchizedek and El.

Of the worlds in succession
And the galaxies in balance,
The Holy One presides:

Ever Triumphant,
Everliving,
Everfresh,
Evertrue,
Forevermore.
My bastion,
My refuge of peace.

Like granite walls of Is-ness,
Or pillars of bronze
Encircling a citadel
With children of peace frolicking within.

Amen.

Native Son Come Home

One in Native Son coalesce.
The grasses, herbage,
Trees' incense.
The swarthy fruits
From trees' largesse.
The swarming gourds
Of God's insects.
The very breeze is
One, enmeshed.

The lightest fragrance
Wafts like smells of
Mating lovers laying.

The fray of hem
Around my neck
Is yours to wear
If clothing's sparse...

The grasses know a sentience,
A life enlivened, enlivening me.

My brother beaver,
Squirrels, raccoons,
And foxes dash
Through fragrant forests
Animated by the force
Illuminating everything.
Selah.

The First Time, Again (Zep Tepi)

Sunscape, Startrace...
The Elements in eloquence,
Brushing fresh wind on skin.

By the river rapids risen
On the wings of a phoenix,
With white light and white fire,
Burning 'cross the galaxy...

Resurrecting the First Time,
The first moments of conception,
The sweet fertility infinitesimal,
The One Oneness
Finding voice in every particle.

Sunscape, Startrace lines in the nexus
For fun and convection,
To season the salt.
To season the season.
Give season to winter,
Give love unto orphans
And praise the Great God.

Photosynthesize and synthesize
All senses to Oneness...
If words should converge,
No thought to their course,
But course with Allah.

Rest assured!
Forged in the force in the center of Suns,
Sprung from the lions of Gargantuan God!

The fabric is soft, course and involved.
Riddles are solved by surrender to All,
Solved by relinquishing search.

Finding the womb of the fruit of the verse,

Finding the root of the fruit of the work,
Finding the truth in Allah.

Wash me clean, Raw,
Like a berry delicious...
Fruit from the verdant hills of Allah.

Fruit from the truth of the prosperous season.
Fruit from the truth of the seed of the teaching,
Imperishable alter to stand and light incense,

Rhythm prescribed as the healing of nations,
Illnesses cleansed,
Tenseness is calmed.

Truth from Brahma on the highest heights glisten,
Streaming with sweat from the radiance of God!

Rushing down the valley to give the gifts freely,
Like a river in the cliffs,
Refreshing parched basins,

The First Time reborn!

Lemon Fresh Water

I thirst and hunger for your fervor,
Your vivacious verse and courage,
Your essential essence and herbage.
Your everlasting love
And lemon fresh water.
The truth from the verdant hills of Allah!

Show me what it is that you wish me to see!

Truth Risen

True Force!
True Fruit!
From the seed,
To the full bloom tree.
300 feet tall overlooking the sea!

Odin from North!
Osiris from South!
To the mouth of The Beast,
Which many run from...

The wellspring springs richness
For spring everlasting.
May everlasting peace,
Envelop the lands.

One God, One People

What names bespeak greatness?
Of the greatest greatness glistening?
Of the Greatest One....
The Holy One...
The Ancient of Ancients.

Of the traditions of Earth,
Enmeshed...
Of the many names and attributes,
Man attributes,
Yet, the Holy One surpasses,
Precedes and stays after, forevermore.

To circumvent the schism
Of religious and regional friction
And draw from the wellspring
With reference to all,
Or all that is known to be a reference to.

Allah, Ahura Mazda, Brahma, the Tao.
El Shaddai, Elohim, Ahia Most High!
Yahweh, The Ultimate, The Allness, Great God!
Amun Ra, Aten, the Kingdom of Osiris...

Eternity, Infinitude, Truth and Pure Essence.
Pure Beauty, for the benefit of all sentient beings!

The most beneficent!
Evermerciful,
Everlasting,
Almighty Evermore!

The mightiest might
On Zion's high heights!
Redeemer of all,
Master teacher of truth!
Oneness itself.
The Holy One...
El Elyon.

Presence, Is-ness, Iam-ness, complete!
The Great Spirit.
The seas of infinity steeped.
The Evermost Everest.
Rest assured of the heavens!
The Holiest Holiness.
The Deepest of Depths.

The most intimate of intimates.
The first and the last.

The unborn,
The self-created,
The Generous One.

The force in the seed.
The guidance of eons.
The laws of the Universe.
The Immutable One.

Praise unto God.
Praise unto the Great God.
Do Maat, Spread Maat,
And praise the Great God!

The purest of pure rare.
The most rarefied!
The densest dank juice,
From the Mother's fresh womb.

The turbulent seas.
The halcyon lakes.
The sweltering forests,
And snow capped peaks.

To merge the four directions
Of the compass, to sphere,
Uniting in the shimmering Sun of Allah!

Praise unto God.

Praise unto the Great God.
Do Maat, Spread Maat,
And praise the Great God!

E. Pluribus Unum

Axum,
Khartoum,
Waset.

Osiris,
Busiris,
Suffice.

Arjuna.
David.
Yosef.

Mohenjo,
Angkor...
Teotihuacan.

Of the wadis of the west,
Beyond the Rocky Mountains' crest.

Beyond the point of no return.
Beyond the moment momentous...

Of the forests in the Congo,
And the steppes in Russian vastland,
To the Indian seas traversed
By Swahili traders.

We bring silk on silt roads,
Washed rich with river water,
Carrying scripture, incense,
Gold and soft cotton.

Underneath the Persian stars
On a plateau conversing,
I dreamt of Asiath consoling my frustration.

The Doorway to the West

Cherry river falls.
Cherry water deep.
Beneath the canyon,
In the cavern.
The cool, coursing current
Like the veins of Earth opened…

Staining shirts with purple fluid.
In the moonlight dripping Blue,
Devouring her flesh…

I began to run off,
Through her fields,
Dripping with a reddened hue,
Like a ripened rose in cherry juice,
Opening the Doorway to the West…

I walked on through
And stood enmeshed,
With cherry flesh…

To the womb of Earth returned,
With cherry orchards spanning acres,
Washing Earth with cherry rivers,
As red as night…

A deeply purple red.
A flood of Mother's blood for nourishing.

Enoch Awakening

Elohim, Ahia High
In the palace pristine
On the throne of the sky.
The Craftsman Supreme.

Blue stones dripping dreams
And the cornerstone goldening,
Deep purple blue
Like an ocean convescing...

Humming blue ozones
Through bones of all beings.

A lion awakens,
But bows before Yah.
An empire rises and falls
Like a dream.
Like a mist of steam
In the ocean of dreams,
And still to stretch endless
Yahweh presides!

The creator of life.
A brilliance unseen.
In Amun it is hidden,
In Ra it is seen.

Yah's brilliance convenes
At every river's mouth,
At every star's nexus,
At every point plotted,
And still it defies
The plotting of points.

Under the shade of the lemon tree dreaming
Elohim plants a seed in the soil with Love.
Enoch awakens...
To walk with God.

On the Mountain Top

On a mountain top singing,
The Glory of Allah!
Let me praise the Great One
In the congregation of faithful...

Let us gather in fields
At first fruit and sing hymns,
Harvesting food and offering oblation!
Finding the plenty in the bounty of Allah!

Allah Hu Akbar!
Allah Hu Akbar!
Allah Hu Akbar!
The Greatest of Greats!

Perseus the pupil,
Donovan the dancer,
Martin the molder,
And Jackson the jumper...

We gather at the mouth of Great River to sing praise!

Allah Hu Akbar!
Allah Hu Akbar!
Allah Hu Akbar!
The Greatest of Greats!

Gather an army for Allah's embrace!
To the hills to make music,
And praise the Great God.
Grow crops,
Raise sheep,
Raise family and praise!

Allah Hu Akbar!
Allah Hu Akbar!
Allah Hu Akbar!
The Greatest of Greats!

The pen on the pad
Engorgeth with dream,
A dream that runs ink
With the love of Allah!

Praise the Great God!
Praise unto the Great God!
Do Maat, Spread Maat,
And praise the Great God!

The Most Melodious One

Arrowroot
Arrow-way
Ariel!
Ariel!

Merge the hemispheres
Unto the Sahel...

Brace for impact
As we meld all mankind,
From the West
To far East entwined...

Whether desert or dense arrangements like Seoul,
The Great God presides over all that unfolds!

The author,
The orchestra, notes and audience,
The music, most melodious masterful tome...
The Book of Life.
All praise unto El Elyon.

Gihon Spring Rising

Babylon abandoned…
For Beit Elyon.

Ergo, the fire on the throne.
The force which permeates stone.
The milk in marrow of bone.

The zone of zones.
The tone of testament,
At home in The Presence.
Living water rising
From frothing wellsprings!

Gihon spring rising
With psalms of the king,
Praising Ahia the highest,
Most Gracious!

Seeing the light of our strivings rise dawned!
Coming home
To Beit Elyon!

Ehyeh Asher Ehyeh

Pasturing the flocks
By holy mount Horeb,
Moshe saw the flame engulfing...

The jewel inside the lotus fold.
The humming eye of El.
The burning lotus bush engulfed,
Ehyeh Asher Ehyeh.

That which is
Could never not,
But always is
Amidst the ought...
I am that which I am is always glowing...
A joy of Yah that never fades.

A joy of jubilance and praise.
All praise unto Ehyeh Asher Ehyeh!

The Word of Jah

New, Eternal Destiny arisen from Hashem,
Life infused with light again…

Jah speaks on mountain peaks,
Seas and seedlings shooting forth.
Jah speaks with reggae beats
Beating in the underground.

The heart of Raphael
Calls compassion down a well
To denizens who've fallen in
To undergrounds,
Shining healing light on wounds…
The power of the Sun is convalescence.

Jah speaks in monsoon winds
Washing in Sri Lankan streets.
Jah speaks in desert tents
Nurturing the sons of Ishmael.

The wanderers walked with thirst
Opening their parched ears
For Jah's rhythmic Nyabingh.

Crystalline songbirds sing
In Ancient Native Midwest Forests,
Calling from a deepened well
Of innocence and brilliance.

Jah speaks in stoic nights
White with snow and crystal ice
Glistening with morning light
Hopeful for the fruit of spring,

To come in times despairingly
The Great Redeemer shined in forth,
Dispelling any cobwebs cornered,
Washing it in revelation…

Revelatory levitating lightning striking Golden Castles,
Channeling the light of
Jah's Golden Guidance!
Awakening in Zion.

Presiding with the silence
Of the early morning redwood forests,
Pregnant with the fertile message
For the subtle wind to copulate with...
Babylon's time is ticking.

Jah speaks in lovers' ears
In early morning rustling,
Nestled in the roses, cherries and
Strawberries of Adam's Eve.

In the evening hour Adam leaves
And picks a fruit from Ancient Trees,
The eyes of Eve's Adam ease
With fruit of Eve's primrose breeze...

Jah speaks in Dedication.

The Healing of the Nations

Oh Almighty!
Of the most Ancient Streams,
Of the Deepest Ravines,
Where Ravens hover wide
With prophetic wings spread…

Where time scales, deeper dilation
Till the infinite is spread
In the interim of one second.

To awaken on her banks
With praise and jubilation!

To gather comrades
For the King's Coronation,
Or rather formal recognition
Of his rule.

For he has reigned
Since before the birth of Time.

Time is his son.
Matter is his son.
All descend from Elohim!

On Raven's wings
Dreams of Zion's bastion rise
From rubble Babylon…

Truth renewing parched landscapes,
Wells of Everliving water well!

Floodgates swell
Like Zion beaming streams of
Revelation 'pon the nations,
Healing every wound.
Selah!

Smelted Seven Times

The forging of a Samurai blade,
For the Love of Elohim
To take me away…
To purify my soul
In the waters of Nu.
To smelt me seven times
In the furnace of Babylon.

Binding true parts to true parts,
And hammering impurities off,
I feel pain.

Stained hands get washed
In the hammering pangs,
As mistakes reveal truth
To the seeker.

I need you El Shaddai!
Without you raving jackals
Reach to take bites,
But you are the holy castle
Of everlasting peace.

I need you more than air,
More than water, more than food.
More than clothing, more than shelter,
More than life itself.

Elohim is my rock,
My redeemer,
My peace.
All praise unto El Elyon!

In the light of your alignment
There is joy, love and fruit.
May all my days be
In the house of Yahweh!

Within the Gates of Zion

Zion's gates
Shoot open like lakes,
With flowing herbs,
Spinaches and watermelons...
Honeydew oozes on shoes
Of God's Children.

Walking in the wilderness
Thorns have stuck in them,
But balms are made ready
For the healing of wounds.

In Zion's gates...
Lithe dancing forms,
Sing jubilant praise to El Elyon...

By the Lute and the Lyre,
By the fire Ahura,
By the morning Ra Rising,
By the tempest of Shiva,
By the winds of The Spirit,
By the Everliving Well
Lovers tell tales
And paint poems with kisses...

Under the Ceiba
A psalm came to him,
And lit him aflame
Like Mount Sinai lightning,
Melting the frost
On frost bitten hands
From Babylon's ice...
In Zion's fair gates
The warmth overflows!

Govinda!
The moon is enlightening.
Looking at you,

Like Yahoshua speaking
The Spirit of Truth…

Govinda!
Your skin is so radiant,
Blue like the ocean
Beneath the deep league…

An archway revealed unto Love has come forth,
Lovers! Abandon the fields of your toil!
To frolic on grasses with honeydew oozing!

We called unto you!
You listened intently.
Guiding us through turbulent seas…
Through dark marshes teeming
With crocodile and hippo,
Smiting Seth and resurrecting Osiris!

Your blue ozones beam streams
Of a Kingdom Supreme,
Of Golden Castles glistening
Atop Zion's peak,
With the Children of God,
From all corners of Earth
Singing praise to the force which animates all.

Selah

Thank You.

The Livity of Light.
The Love of Universalism,
Beyond the Ism,
The Is-ness of light.
Massaging every contour,
Turning us towards truth.

I bow to you Immensity.
I bow to you Elaha,
The Most Ancient of Ancients.

I bow to your Everlasting Arc,
The torque of galaxies sparked
From the deepness of your wisdom.

The pristine palace glistens,
Shining insight through the seas.
The living well swelling
With the ripest nectarines.
The fountainhead's commencement…
The source of all manifestation.

Thank you, Great One.
Great Golden Gong.
Great Wisdom of the Embers.
Great Magnitude of Roots.
Thank you.

The Fountainhead

The wind through the trees
Sounds like a running stream
Off the brooks of Arnon
Through the valley gorge!

From Yamuna to Amazon,
From python to eagle,
From valley grass to mountainhead,
Elaha reigns strong!

The force of forces,
The Fountainhead!
The one force which surfaces
Bubbling from Iam-ness.

Great grandfather of thought.
Great Oneness perfuse,
The One Force enlivening,
Animating all…

The force of altitudes.
The force in seeds sprouting.
The force in Suns fusing.
The force in rivers rushing…

The force in all wind,
All wind washing forests…

What is once well done
Has been done,
It is One!

One Great God presides, timeless,
In an infinite tumbling,
Every object confides in!

Redwood, Beechwood,
All come from The Root!

The tree of life sprung
By the will of Elaha!

The orange lotus blossom
Spawning in night,
Blooming in the rays
Of New Born Sunlight!

Elaha! Elaha!
Elaha the Great!
Great Gates of the Deep.
Great Fountain of Fruit.
Great Lakes of Fish Flopping.
Great Source of all Truth.

All praise is due unto you, Great Elaha.

Selah.

Information About the Author:

Johnathan Abraham Antelept is the Founder, Owner and CEO of STONE OF XAVIER LLC.

Contact Information:

johnathan.antelept@stoneofxavier.com